People in My Community

Mail Carrier

by JoAnn Early Macken
Photographs by Gregg Andersen

Reading consultant: Susan Nations, M.Ed., author/literacy coach/consultant

WEEKLY WR READER®
EARLY LEARNING LIBRARY

Please visit our web site at: **www.earlyliteracy.cc**
For a free color catalog describing Weekly Reader® Early Learning Library's
list of high-quality books, call 1-877-445-5824 (USA) or 1-800-387-3178 (Canada).
Weekly Reader® Early Learning Library's fax: (414) 336-0164.

Library of Congress Cataloging-in-Publication Data

Macken, JoAnn Early, 1953-
    Mail carrier / by JoAnn Early Macken.
      p. cm. — (People in my community)
    Summary: Photographs and simple text describe the work done by mail carriers.
    Includes bibliographical references and index.
    ISBN 0-8368-3590-5 (lib. bdg.)
    ISBN 0-8368-3597-2 (softcover)
    1. Letter carriers—United States—Juvenile literature. [1. Letter carriers. 2. Occupations.]
I. Title. II. Series.
HE6499.M13   2003
383'.145'02373—dc21
                                                                2002032961

First published in 2003 by
Weekly Reader® Early Learning Library
330 West Olive Street, Suite 100
Milwaukee, WI 53212 USA

Copyright © 2003 by Weekly Reader® Early Learning Library

Art direction: Tammy Gruenewald
Page layout: Katherine A. Goedheer
Photographer: Gregg Andersen
Editorial assistant: Diane Laska-Swanke

Printed in the United States of America

1 2 3 4 5 6 7 8 9 07 06 05 04 03

Note to Educators and Parents

Reading is such an exciting adventure for young children! They are beginning to integrate their oral language skills with written language. To encourage children along the path to early literacy, books must be colorful, engaging, and interesting; they should invite the young reader to explore both the print and the pictures.

People in My Community is a new series designed to help children read about the world around them. In each book young readers will learn interesting facts about some familiar community helpers.

Each book is specially designed to support the young reader in the reading process. The familiar topics are appealing to young children and invite them to read — and re-read — again and again. The full-color photographs and enhanced text further support the student during the reading process.

In addition to serving as wonderful picture books in schools, libraries, homes, and other places where children learn to love reading, these books are specifically intended to be read within an instructional guided reading group. This small group setting allows beginning readers to work with a fluent adult model as they make meaning from the text. After children develop fluency with the text and content, the book can be read independently. Children and adults alike will find these books supportive, engaging, and fun!

— Susan Nations, M.Ed., author, literacy coach,
and consultant in literacy development

The mail carrier
delivers letters
and packages.

Mail carriers sort the mail at the post office before they deliver it.

Each letter and package must go to the right **address**. Do you know your address?

address

Some mail carriers walk to deliver the mail. They might carry the mail in a **pouch**. They might push the mail in a cart.

pouch

Some mail carriers drive cars or **trucks** to deliver the mail. They drive from house to house.

truck

2208844

Mail carriers walk or drive the same route each day. They deliver mail to homes, schools, and businesses.

Mail carriers wear blue **uniforms**. In the summer, they may wear shorts.

uniform

UNITED STATES
POSTAL SERVICE

In the winter, they wear warmer clothes. Mail carriers work in all kinds of weather.

Isn't it fun to get something in the mail?

Glossary

address — the place where a letter or package is to be delivered

route — a line of travel

sort — to put in order

uniform — clothing worn by members of a group such as police officers, firefighters, or mail carriers

For More Information

Fiction Books

Lillegard, Dee. *Tortoise Brings the Mail.*
New York: Dutton Children's Books, 1997.

Nonfiction Books

Flanagan, Alice K. *Here Comes Mr. Eventoff with the Mail.* New York: Children's Press, 1999.

Kottke, Jan. *A Day with a Mail Carrier.*
New York: Children's Press, 2000.

Maynard, Christopher. *Jobs People Do.*
New York: Dorling Kindersley, 2001.

Ready, Dee. *Mail Carriers.*
Mankato, Minn.: Bridgestone Books, 1998.

Web Sites
What Does a Letter Carrier Do?
www.whatdotheydo.com/letter_c.htm
A girl goes to work with her mother, a letter carrier

Index

About the Author

JoAnn Early Macken is the author of children's poetry, two rhyming picture books, *Cats on Judy* and *Sing-Along Song,* and various other nonfiction series. She teaches children to write poetry and received the Barbara Juster Esbensen 2000 Poetry Teaching Award. JoAnn is a graduate of the MFA in Writing for Children Program at Vermont College. She lives in Wisconsin with her husband and their two sons.